AEI SPECIAL ANALYSIS
*Timely examinations of issues be[...]
in the formulation of public [policy]*

The Multilateral Trade Negotiations

Toward Greater Liberalization?

Robert E. Baldwin

AMERICAN ENTERPRISE INSTITUTE
for Public Policy Research
Washington, D.C.

Robert E. Baldwin is professor of economics at the University of Wisconsin-Madison and a frequent witness before congressional committees investigating trade matters. Professor Baldwin served as the first chief economist in the Office of Special Trade Representative (STR) in 1963–1964. He has since been a consultant on trade policy issues with STR, the World Bank, the U.S. Department of Labor, the United Nations Conference on Trade and Development, the U.S. Chamber of Commerce, and the Committee for Economic Development. He is the author of numerous articles and several books in the field of international trade, including *Nontariff Distortions of International Trade*, the well-known Brookings volume.

ISBN 0-8447-1082-2

Library of Congress Catalog Card No. 79-2454

Special Analysis No. 79-2

Printed in the United States of America

Price $3 per copy

CONTENTS

1

Introduction

As the Multilateral Trade Negotiations (also known as the Tokyo Round) draw to a conclusion, the U.S. Congress faces a significant choice; it can either accept or reject without amendment a proposed set of rules of "good" behavior in international commerce that will shape the conduct of international trade for at least the rest of this century. The rules were drawn up in more than five years of negotiations aimed both at further cutting tariffs and at reducing or eliminating nontariff impediments to and distortions of international trade. Ministers of the ninety-nine nations involved agreed in the inaugural Tokyo Declaration that where the reduction or elimination of such nontariff impediments was not appropriate they should at least be brought "under more effective international discipline."

The emphasis on nontariff distortions of trade makes the current negotiating round different from the six previous trade-liberalizing exercises held since World War II within the framework of the General Agreement on Tariffs and Trade (GATT). Earlier negotiations focused primarily on reducing tariffs. The last multilateral effort, the so-called Kennedy Round lasting from 1962 to 1967, cut import duties in the major industrial nations by an average of 35 percent for dutiable manufactures and 20 percent for agricultural products. As a result, the average duty for dutiable manufactured goods declined to only about 10 percent in the United States, the European Community, and Japan by the conclusion of the Kennedy Round cuts. This is in contrast to a U.S. tariff level for dutiable imports of nearly 60 percent in 1931. Further tariff reductions of about 33 percent for all participants are scheduled as part of the agreements reached in the Tokyo Round negotiations.

The most significant part of these agreements, however, is the series of detailed codes spelling out permissible and nonpermissible "good" behavior by governments in almost all areas where nontariff measures have threatened the basic trade-liberalizing objective of the GATT. Consideration of these codes is especially timely not merely because the negotiations have just ended but also because, unlike tariff reductions, the codes must be approved by both houses of Congress before they can be implemented. The implementing bill will not only approve the agreements and any administrative actions needed to implement them but will repeal and amend any existing laws that must be changed for them to take effect. In accordance with the 1974 Trade Act, no amendments to the implementing bill will be permitted in either the House or

Senate, and the bill must be voted on no more than ninety legislation days from its introduction in Congress.[1] According to present plans, the President will submit the implementing bill to Congress in May.

The purpose of this analysis is to assist in evaluating the results of the Tokyo Round, especially the package agreement on nontariff measures. This package covers subsidies and countervailing duties, anti-dumping practices, government procurement policies, valuation and licensing practices, technical barriers to trade (standards), differential and more favorable treatment for developing countries, safeguard actions for balance of payments and developmental purposes, and dispute settlement and surveillance procedures under the GATT. The negotiators failed to reach agreement on codes covering safeguards against injurious imports and commercial counterfeiting, but the hope is that final agreement on these subjects will be reached within a few months. Moreover, the participants agreed to reassess in the near future the GATT provisions relating to export restraints. In addition, specific agreements have been reached with regard to steel, aircraft, certain agricultural products, and several nontariff measures of only bilateral interest. The following analysis will describe the measures or practices that have led to the desire for improved codes, the nature of the agreed upon or proposed codes and how they differ from existing GATT rules, and finally a brief evaluation of each. After appraising the mechanisms established to secure compliance with the different nontariff codes, the various other agreements concluded will be examined more closely, including the tariff-cutting formula that has been adopted. However, prior to analyzing the codes and other agreements in detail, the paper presents a general overview of the Tokyo Round that considers whether this negotiation promises a period of greater trade liberalization or one of greater control over world trade.

2

Toward Greater Liberalization?

Whether international commerce will become less or more distorted by governmental measures as a result of the recently concluded trade negotiations depends on two related factors: the negotiated agreements themselves and the various measures adopted in securing the initial negotiating authority, in maintaining domestic support during the negotiations, in "selling" the negotiating results to legislators and the public, and finally in implementing the results.

Consideration of the negotiated agreements by themselves leads to the conclusion that the scope and detail of the new nontariff codes represent a brilliant accomplishment. Although trade officials in national capitals and Geneva have frequently complained about nontariff barriers over the last fifteen years, most have reacted rather negatively to negotiations on these barriers, protesting that "they are too complicated to deal with in a multilateral setting"; "we don't have any, so what is there to negotiate?" and "the GATT already provides as much detail on the subject as is feasible." At the outset of the current negotiation these statements seemed to typify the positions of most delegations. At best, progress in only one or two technical areas appeared possible. However, in large part because of the imagination and persistence of U.S. negotiators and their supporting personnel (in both the current and previous administrations), a sweeping elaboration and partial revision has been achieved in almost every major article of the GATT. To many people's surprise, the closer the negotiators looked at the various articles with a view to updating and clarifying them, the more they found that they could be improved. The means employed to accomplish this was ingenious. Rather than trying to revise the Articles of Agreement or add new ones, interpretive codes were developed that need not be signed by all GATT members. Moreover, countries who are not GATT members may become signatories.

The various technical codes covering standards, customs valuation, licensing, and commercial counterfeiting may not bring about any large increase in trade, but they will certainly reduce many irritations that worsen international relations. The government procurement code is mainly technical, but for most of the industrial countries (including the United States) it represents a basic liberalizing change in trade policy. Not only is it consistent with fundamental notions of "fairness" in international trade but it can increase U.S. exports considerably. As will be explained in some detail in the next chapter, the new (or proposed) agreements covering subsidies, anti-dumping practices, safeguards, differential and more favorable treatment for developing countries, and dispute settlement procedures offer the opportunity for halting the trend toward inward-looking protectionist policies and of restoring a greater degree of order in international commerce. However, as a part of the compromising processes of any negotiation, language has been accepted in these codes that makes it uncertain as to whether this opportunity will be realized. For example, if in the implementation of the subsidies code decisions relating to "serious prejudice," "nullification or impairment," and "injury to a domestic industry" are made along the same lines as in the recent past, trade-distorting subsidies will continue to grow. Since the code is designed only "to apply fully and to interpret" Articles VI, XVI, and XXIII, some GATT members may insist that nothing very much should change from the past. Specifying in more detail the procedures to be followed in initiating and continuing safeguard actions without, however, coming to grips with the adjustment problem may also not produce any significant liberalization in this field. Similarly, the failure to change the dispute settlement procedures other than by establishing many more committees and potential panels as well as the lack of a procedure or set of criteria for the "graduation" of the developing countries to fuller GATT responsibilities could block significant trade-liberalizing changes in these areas. In the area of tariffs, the average duty reduction of about 33 percent is a positive liberalization sign, but the complete or partial exclusion from the general duty-cutting formula of many items of export interest to the developing countries is very disappointing to these nations. The failure to ease the many quantitative restrictions affecting the exports of these countries magnifies this disappointment. For such reasons, it is not yet clear whether the developing countries will sign the various nontariff agreements.

There are, as is well known, many important individuals and groups within governments and in the private sectors of the major industrial trading nations that do not wish to liberalize trade. These people employ such code words as "managed free trade," "fair trade," and "orderly growth" to mask the basic idea that the government should play a greater, not a lesser, role in restricting international trade. This approach is justified as preventing even more restrictive government actions, meeting an oversupply situation that is sometimes "temporary" and other times "chronic," offsetting governmental or private actions in other countries, and dealing with the "realities" of "bigness" and "interdependence" in the world. This is not the place to present in detail the merits of trade liberalization, since that has been done many times by others.[2] But an abundance of evidence indicates that greater government intervention in the trade field increases rather than reduces international economic disputes and, more important, decreases the long-run efficiency and growth of nations.

The possibility exists that the new codes could become a means of furthering the goal of "managed free trade." This can be seen in part from such Tokyo Round results as the new International Steel Committee, the discriminatory features of the proposed safeguards code and its lack of attention to adjustment issues, the implicit acceptance of permanent domestic subsidies for almost any reason, and the continued cartelization of international agriculture. But more important than these features of the Tokyo Round agreements are recent governmental measures taken outside of the negotiations, such as the tightening of textile quotas.

Observers of public policy usually seem to conclude that the existence of ongoing trade negotiations acts to reduce the likelihood that protectionist measures will be adopted. This may not be true, however, especially for the recent negotiations. When a president decides to launch a major trade negotiation, it is essential for his domestic and international prestige that the bill giving him authority to do so be passed by Congress. One might think, therefore, that presidents would carefully canvass Congress to discover what price they must pay for congressional support, but this is not always done. Thus, once the president is committed to the broad goal of holding a negotiation, he is usually forced to pay a protectionist price for the support of key legislative groups. President Eisenhower accepted the imposition of oil quotas in the late 1950s as part of the price of gaining support for extensions of the reciprocal trade program; President Kennedy agreed to seek a formal international agreement permitting import quotas for cotton textiles at the time the Trade Expansion Act of 1962 was under consideration; and President Nixon agreed to extend the textile agreement to cover man-made fibers and wool at the time the Trade Act of 1974 was being considered. Of course, these protectionist pressures did not arise merely in response to the consideration of these new trade bills. But it is difficult for legislators to attach provisions favoring particular trade interests to a nontrade bill to which the president is also committed. Their attempt to push through a specific piece of trade legislation favoring these trade interests risks such a large scale "piggyback" effort on the part of other protectionist groups that the president is almost sure to have to veto the bill.

As pointed out in the introduction, the current negotiations differ from others in that the nontariff codes, which are the most important part of the agreements reached, must be approved by Congress. Moreover, once negotiations are under way the president is deeply committed to a negotiating "success," since failure would damage his international and domestic image. Thus, he is again forced to pay a protectionist price to ensure congressional endorsement of the agreements. The manner in which the price has been extracted thus far is quite interesting. Under the Trade Act of 1974 the secretary of Treasury was empowered to waive the imposition of countervailing duties, if he determined that there was a reasonable prospect of success for a trade agreement providing for the reduction or elimination of subsidized imports. This authority was utilized, but it expired January 4, 1979, one year before the trade negotiating authority of the 1974 act ends. Moreover, Congress failed to extend the authority in the closing days of the last Congress. Since the European Community and other participants refused to conclude the negotiations unless the waiver was extended, the administration made the extension a priority item in its legislative program. This situation provided a near perfect opportunity for protectionist interests to maximize their leverage in Congress.

The waiver extension passed the House (and, later, the Senate) easily, but only after the Ways and Means Committee was satisfied that an agreement between the administration and the textile industry on textile imports had been worked out. The resulting agreement, entitled the Administration Textile Program, begins by stating that the administration "is determined to assist the beleaguered textile and apparel industry and is committed to its health and growth." Among the specific pledges are actions to "tighten controls for the remaining life" of existing agreements under the Multifiber Arrangement, including a restriction on the ability of an exporter to carry over unfilled quotas from one year to the next. When necessary "to preclude further disruption" the administration also will aim at holding 1979 imports to 1978 levels.

The sugar industry also benefited from the need to pass the waiver bill. A proposal raising sugar prices had been attached to the waiver bill that failed in the fading hours of the last Congress. Apparently believing that the sugar lobby also had to be satisfied before the waiver bill could be passed, the administration proposed raising the domestic price per pound eight-tenths of a cent to 15.8 cents (the world price is about 8.5 cents a pound) plus paying a subsidy of a half cent a pound.

The price of the steel industry for support of the waiver bill and the package agreement reportedly has been the establishment of the new International Steel Committee in OECD and continuation of the "trigger price" system for steel imports. The steel import penetration ratio dropped from 22 percent in May 1978 to about 14 percent in December 1978, while the industry has operated at about 90 percent of capacity during 1979. Since last November the President has also approved affirmative International Trade Commission findings of injury to domestic producers in the cases of industrial fasteners of iron or steel, high carbon ferrochromium, and clothespins; removed over $3.9 billion worth of manufactured goods from the duty-free preference arrangement for developing countries, while adding only $0.2 billion worth of new products to the preference list; and extended import quotas introduced under an orderly marketing agreement on colored TV sets to include Taiwan and South Korea in addition to Japan.

Additional opportunities for adopting protective measures exist in formulating the means to implement the new nontariff agreements. The 1974 Trade Act requires that the nontariff trade agreements be referred for consideration to the appropriate House and Senate committees dealing with the issues involved. This resulted, for example, in members of the House Subcommittee on Small Business threatening to withhold their support of the government procurement code because some minority citizens operating small businesses might lose government procurement contracts. Although net exports and employment of all firms taken together would rise considerably as a result of the agreement, interest groups that might lose under the agreement were not persuaded to give up their fight for protection. As a result of these protectionist pressures, the government procurement agreement was renegotiated so that it now does not apply "to set-asides on behalf of small and minority businesses." The cost of this was an equivalent withdrawal of liberalizing procurement concessions by other countries. Another instance where greater protectionism may occur as part of the implementation process relates to the complaint by a number of industry groups that the Treasury is not strict enough in determining the existence of foreign subsidization and dumping by other countries. Consequently, as part of an effort to establish a new Department of Trade, some members of Congress may propose that the International Trade Commission should determine not only whether injury results from dumping (as the commission now does) but whether subsidization or dumping are occurring. Such a charge would undoubtedly be interpreted by other countries as a further protectionist move by the United States.

The protectionist costs of the Tokyo Round negotiation thus appear to be considerable. The traditional liberal-trade business and public-interest groups have not mounted an effective countercampaign against the protectionist interests. Furthermore, as the Smoot-Hawley Tariff of 1930 vividly demonstrated, when the Congress becomes too deeply involved in the details of trade negotiations as distinguished from broad overall trade policy, protectionism is highly likely. This is not the fault of individual members who are only trying to carry out the wishes of their constituents. The collective effect of their actions, however, is to adopt (or pressure the president into adopting) measures that are not always in the interest of the nation as a whole. Recent actions with regard to the Tokyo Round agreements seem to illustrate this.

What conclusions should be drawn about the Tokyo Round agreements from this analysis of the favorable and unfavorable features of the negotiations? As the various interest groups pressuring for special treatment know very well, in the short run it is important for international political relations that Congress approve the nontariff trade agreements and the changes necessary to implement them. Not to do so would be highly damaging to the leadership role of the United States. Although the protectionist costs that have already been paid to get an implementing bill introduced are disturbing, nothing can be done about them at this stage. But every effort should be made by public-interest groups to minimize further concessions of this type.

In the longer run, the possibility of restoring greater international order and consensus within a liberal framework of world trade seems very much worth the downside risk that the agreements may lead to a less dynamic, inward-looking international trade environment. But if the liberal-trade goal is to be implemented and the Multilateral Trade Negotiations are to go down in history as a forward rather than backward step in expanding world trade on a rational basis and in promoting international political stability, it is necessary that private groups and the government make every effort to see that the codes are enforced. It is necessary to ensure not only that industries receiving protection are really in need of it and are attempting to adjust to import competition but also that vigorous efforts are made both to eliminate foreign subsidies that injure U.S. firms and to reduce foreign discrimination in government purchasing policies. In other words, contrary to what protectionist interests sometimes allege, a liberal trade policy does not mean being "soft" on rule violations. On the contrary, it means adhering closely to agreed upon rules in an open and fair manner. If such a policy is to have a chance of succeeding, the U.S. government must actively promote it within the GATT as well as on the domestic scene. Periodic efforts must be made, for example, to improve the codes and extend their coverage. Moreover, there are several areas of trade policy, such as export restrictions, trading by state enterprises, and trade in services, where new and improved rules of "good" behavior are needed. Finally, a not inconsequential aspect of implementing the trade agreements in a liberal manner is to be sure that technically competent and impartial individuals fill the various administrative positions dealing with trade policies within the U.S. government as well as within the GATT and other international organizations.

3

The Nontariff Agreements

While a general appraisal of the Tokyo Round negotiations must entail the consideration of all related trade policies adopted over the last five years, a full appreciation of the accomplishments and failures of these negotiations also requires a detailed analysis of the various agreements reached on nontariff measures. The purpose of this chapter is to present such an analysis.

Subsidies and Countervailing Duties

Two trends of recent years have been especially important in focusing attention on the potential trade-distorting effects of subsidies. One is the increasing economic intervention by governments in order to redistribute income toward various groups that the electorate regards as "socially deserving," while the other is the growing degree of openness and interdependence among the major trading nations. As a result, there are many more types of government subsidies than when the GATT was first adopted, and any given subsidy is now likely to have a more direct effect on trade than in the late 1940s.

Selective subsidies that affect production activities, that is, those that are not merely lump-sum income transfers, tend to misallocate economic resources and thereby reduce the potential output of the international community unless the subsidies serve to offset other economic distortions that cannot be eliminated or handled by better means. There are, in fact, a number of circumstances where subsidies can be justified on this ground. For example, some types of socially desirable research may not take place if a firm fears that the results will become freely available to its competitors and make it impossible to recoup the costs of undertaking the research. Similarly, the stickiness of wages along with imperfections of capital markets may justify temporary subsidies to particular regions or specific industries. But if the reason for the subsidy is to promote economic efficiency and growth, the subsidy should be only temporary. However, one may wish to assist a particular group simply on equity grounds or for some other noneconomic reason. Moreover, various political or social factors may prevent the government from providing direct income grants that do not distort production. In these circumstances international political and economic problems often arise because distorting production may produce not just temporary but permanent income losses to citizens of other countries.

Article III of the GATT explicitly permits "the payment of subsidies exclusively to domestic producers." However, Article XVI requires that members who maintain a subsidy "which operates directly or indirectly to increase exports . . . or reduce imports . . . shall notify the Contracting Parties . . . of the estimated effects of the subsidization."[3] If "it is determined that serious prejudice to the interests of any contracting party is caused or threatened by such subsidization," the country granting the subsidy "shall, upon request, discuss . . . the possibility of limiting the subsidization." In 1955 a section added to the article stated that any subsidy on the export of a nonprimary product resulting "in the sale of such product for export at a price lower than the comparable price charged . . . in the domestic market" should cease after January 1958 or "the earliest practicable date thereafter." At the insistence of the United States export subsidies on primary products, that is, agricultural products and minerals, were not prohibited, although they were not to give a member "more than an equitable share of world export trade" in the affected product.

While open and direct export subsidy of manufactured goods by the advanced industrial countries has been kept to a minimum since the late 1950s, various indirect subsidies have developed that the new code tries to control more effectively. First it strengthens the GATT condemnation of government export subsidies on nonprimary products by stating flatly that they should not be granted. This ban is also extended to minerals. More important, by eliminating the requirement that export subsidies result in a lower sales price abroad than at home, it recognizes that under conditions of imperfect competition export subsidies need not always result in dual pricing. An updated list of export subsidies is also provided that includes such measures as currency retention schemes, internal freight rates more favorable for export goods than for domestic products, and special tax, credit, and insurance-rate breaks for exporters. However, export tax benefits such as those provided when U.S. firms form a Domestic International Sales Corporation (DISC) may still be permitted under these latter rules, and the financing of exports at only slightly more than the government's borrowing rate will definitely still be allowed.

In carrying out their wide-ranging efforts for income redistribution and full employment, governments provide extensive domestic subsidies for specific industries, for example, coal, steel, shipping and shipbuilding, textiles, aircraft, and electronics; for specific regions, such as depressed areas; and even for broad product sectors and activities, for example, manufacturing, agriculture, education, health services, and research. The subsidizing means include favorable tax treatment (tax holidays and deferrals, accelerated depreciation, investment credits), below-market borrowing privileges, the payment of fringe benefits, production subsidies, wage subsidies, lump-sum payments, and the sale of government-owned services at favorable rates. It does not take an economist to appreciate that domestic firms receiving this kind of assistance are able to compete more effectively against foreign imports and also in export markets.

As already noted, Article XVI of the GATT provides for consultation only if a member believes another's subsidies are seriously prejudicing its interests. An alternative route for settling such disputes is the use of Article XXIII, which relates to "nullification or impairment" of benefits accruing under the General Agreement. If a contracting party considers that any of these benefits is being nullified or impaired, it can, after the failure of bilateral consultations, have the matter referred to the contracting parties as a whole. Over time the procedure has evolved of appointing a working party or panel of experts to investigate the dispute and report on the merits of the alleged nullification or impairment in terms of the Articles of Agreement. After receiving the report the contracting parties can, if they deem the circumstances warrant it, authorize one of the parties to suspend concessions it has granted to the offending party. The use of the panel or working party to settle disputes has been infrequent, however. Between 1948 and 1977 only thirty-five disputes of all types reached this stage, and their frequency has diminished sharply in recent years.[4]

The greater use of domestic subsidies in most industrial countries other than the United States coupled with the vagueness of existing GATT provisions covering subsidies and the inadequate mechanism for dispute settlement prompted the United States to press in the Tokyo Round negotiations for substantial changes in the rules on domestic subsidies. The code that has evolved explicitly recognizes the right of signatories to use domestic subsidies "for the promotion of social and economic policy objectives," including the elimination of industrial, economic, and social disadvantages of specific regions, the restructuring of certain sectors adversely affected by trade and other economic policies, the maintenance of employment, and the encouragement of research and development programs. It also lists means of subsidization (with the implication that they are legitimate and need not be temporary) to meet these objectives, such as government financing of commerical enterprises, government provision of operational services to these enterprises, government financing of research, and various fiscal incentives to private firms. The code also explicitly recognizes, however, that domestic subsidies may cause or threaten to cause serious prejudice, especially when they adversely affect "the conditions of normal competition," and the signatories agree to seek to avoid causing such injury. Moreover, the dispute settlement mechanism is improved for both export and domestic subsidies. If consultations with other members fail to satisfy a signatory who believes another nation's domestic subsidy causes injury to its own domestic industry, nullification or impairment of its GATT benefits, or serious prejudice to its interests, the dispute can be referred to a committee of signatories of the code for conciliation. If the matter remains unresolved, any signatory involved can request that the committee appoint a panel of experts to present its findings concerning the rights and obligations of the parties involved. The committee may then authorize appropriate countermeasures based on the panel's report.

For countries that subsidize more extensively than the United States, the incentive to agree to tighter controls over both export and domestic subsidies is to obtain an "injury clause" in the U.S. countervailing duty law. Countervailing duties are discriminatory levies on imported goods permitted under the GATT (Article VI) to offset any government subsidy on the "manufacture, production or export of any merchandise" if the effect of the subsidy is "to cause or threaten material injury" to a domestic industry. Imposing countervailing duties to handle the problem of foreign subsidies is quite different from utilizing the provisions of Articles XVI and XXIII. The countervailing-duty route can be used only against subsidized imports, since imposing import duties obviously does not offset a country's loss of an export market because of foreign subsidies. More important, the decision whether to countervail is made entirely by the importing country according to its established procedures. Other countries have been concerned for many years because U.S. procedures do not require proof of material injury before countervailing duties can be imposed on subsidized imports. However, U.S. negotiators agreed to accept the normal GATT requirement that material injury must be caused or threatened before countervailing can take place. Nevertheless, provisional countervailing measures can be taken after a preliminary finding that a subsidy exists and there is sufficient evidence of injury. The criteria listed in the code for determining injury also specify that the effects of the subsidy on the volume of imports as well as their price must be taken into consideration.

One might conclude from the language of the subsidies/countervailing duty code that the United States will not receive any benefits that do not already exist in the various GATT articles dealing with subsidies, even though the country is giving up its right to countervail without proof of material injury and may be implicitly accepting the legitimacy of many domestic subsidies of other countries. A more appropriate view, in my opinion, is that the code represents a potentially significant accomplishment that may enable the international community to control in a realistic manner the trade-distorting effects of domestic subsidies, particularly those that reduce the exports of another country. The United States has never literally enforced its own subsidy and countervailing duty law; to do so would create an administrative nightmare and lead to such extensive retaliation that our international economic and political position would be jeopardized. On the other hand, the various provisions of the GATT that apply to subsidies, especially to domestic subsidies, are vague and scattered throughout the document. Moreover, the dispute settlement mechanism under Article XXIII is more a means of resolving unusual situations not covered by the specific articles of the agreement than a regular procedure for settling ordinary disputes that arise in the operation of trade policies. Consequently, it has been difficult to find a sensible intermediate position between countervailing against every trivial foreign subsidy and ignoring all but the most flagrant trade-distorting subsidies. The introduction of an injury clause into U.S. law coupled with the creation of a dispute settlement committee for subsidies alone may enable us to attain such a position. The word "may" is used because the key to the code's success is how effective the dispute settlement and enforcement mechanism will be. Since this issue applies to all the codes, it will be considered later in this chapter.

ANTI-DUMPING PRACTICES

One of the few areas of progress on nontariff measures in the Kennedy Round was agreement on a code dealing with anti-dumping practices. The United States signed the document as an Executive Agreement, but the Congress strongly objected to the fact that it was never submitted to that body for approval. A law was passed directing the International Trade Commission to ignore the new code in making its decisions on whether injury occurred as a result of dumping. The new anti-dumping agreement reached in the Tokyo Round affords an opportunity to eliminate this highly unsatisfactory state of affairs, since it will be part of the package submitted to Congress for approval and the implementing bill will contain any necessary changes in U.S. law.

The new agreement on the implementation of anti-dumping practices under Article VI of GATT differs from the previous one mainly in two respects: the determination of injury and the establishment of a dispute settlement mechanism. The impetus for revision of the anti-dumping code was the desire to make its injury provisions consistent with those negotiated in the code on subsidies and countervailing duties. Like those in the latter code, the provisions of the new agreement specify that both the volume of dumped imports and their effect on prices in domestic markets be considered in determining injury. The illustrative list of factors to consider in examining the impact of dumping on the industry concerned is made consistent with the subsidies code, as is the provision cautioning that demonstrated injury under the code must be caused by dumped imports rather than other economic factors. Both the subsidies/countervailing duties and anti-dumping codes state in footnotes that "injury" is to mean material injury to a domestic industry. However, the revised U.S. anti-dumping law to be submitted as part of the implementing bill apparently will simply specify that injury not be "immaterial" rather than use the phrase "material injury."

Although a committee on anti-dumping practices had been established under the old code, its purpose had been merely to facilitate periodic consultations among members on matters relating to the administration of anti-

13

dumping systems. The new agreement makes the powers of the committee similar to those of committees established under the other nontariff codes. It can perform a conciliation role in disputes, appoint panels to examine the matters under dispute, and authorize retaliatory actions.

SAFEGUARDS

Article XIX of the General Agreement permits member countries to withdraw or modify a concession (such as a tariff reduction) previously granted "if, as a result of unforeseen developments," a product is being imported in such increased quantities "as to cause or threaten serious injury to domestic producers." But consultations with exporting countries must take place prior to or immediately after the withdrawal or modification and, if equivalent concessions on other products are not agreed upon, these exporting countries can withdraw some of their own concessions.

These "escape clauses" or safeguards have not worked well in recent years. Most of the major industrial trading nations have entered into various bilateral agreements with other countries outside the GATT framework, whereby these other countries "voluntarily" agree to limit their exports of particular products. This procedure permits the importing country to discriminate against the exports of one or more countries and does not involve the granting of offsetting concessions by the importing nation. The exporting nations have not complained of "nullification and impairment" under Article XXIII because of the threat of even more severe restriction if the matter gets into the hands of national legislators.

A draft code under consideration attempts to bring the various types of safeguards back within the GATT framework and to spell out in more detail the procedures each country must follow in carrying out such actions. On the latter point, the code sets forth (as the relevant U.S. law does) a list of indicators to be considered in determining serious injury and also specifies that safeguard measures should be only temporary and progressively liberalized. A committee on safeguard measures, composed of the signatories to this code, is also established for surveillance and dispute settlement. Whether a country will have the right to restrict imports from only a few sources—that is, to discriminate against certain countries—and whether "voluntary" export restraints and "orderly" marketing agreements will be allowed under Article XIX is still under discussion. Reportedly, the European Community is strongly urging that selective discrimination be permitted. The developing countries, on the other hand, are vigorously opposing the proposal, since they believe it will be used mainly against them for both economic and political purposes.

The most-favored-nation principle (MFN), that is, nondiscrimination among countries with respect to trade policies, has already been so widely

14

breached that it is somewhat hard to become concerned about a limited policy of selectivity. For example, the European Community discriminates against nonmembers such as the United States. The EC also gives special preferential treatment to the former colonies of its members as well as to several other states. Both of these actions are permitted under current GATT rules. There are other customs unions and free trade areas in the world, including, for example, the arrangement between the United States and Canada on automobiles and automobile parts. The granting of tariff preferences to the developing countries and the fact that the new codes will discriminate against nonsignatories are further indications that the most-favored-nation principle is widely violated in actual practice.

More important than the MFN principle is whether economic adjustments occur in the injured industry so that the import restrictions are in fact only temporary. Unless solid evidence of adjustment efforts is required, the same conditions justifying the initial relief are likely to persist for years. Under these circumstances it is difficult, as experience with textiles indicates, not to find some way of continuing the import relief. If pressures were exerted on industries that resulted in the gradual movement of resources out of these sectors into more productive lines, the matter of temporary discrimination would not seem so significant. Unfortunately, neither U.S. law nor GATT rules deal effectively with the adjustment problem.

GOVERNMENT PROCUREMENT

Purchasing policies by governments are excluded from the GATT principle of nondiscrimination under Article III. But favoritism toward domestic producers in government nonmilitary purchasing has increasingly irritated exporters as government purchases have escalated in recent years. The United States discriminates against foreign exporters on the basis of the so-called Buy American Act of 1933.[5] It has been implemented by generally giving U.S. producers a 6 percent price preference over foreigners. However, small firms and those in depressed areas receive a 12 percent price preference, and the Defense Department gives U.S. producers a 50 percent preference on all nonmilitary purchases. Many states and municipalities in the United States also have purchasing rules that openly discriminate against foreigners. Other countries do not have such explicitly discriminating legislation, but this does not mean that they do not favor their domestic producers over foreign bidders. A study of the share of domestic purchases in total nonmilitary spending by governments suggests that by using various administrative means other nations are every bit as discriminatory as the United States.[6]

Stating in a code that governments should not discriminate against foreign products or suppliers in their purchasing policies is obviously merely a first step. Discrimination is the result not only of deliberate efforts to favor local producers but also of ignorance on the part of purchasing agents who are reluctant to spend the time and take the risks involved in purchasing from foreign suppliers. Consequently, it is necessary for nations to establish administrative procedures that enable foreigners to learn about and participate in bidding opportunities, meet the required specifications, find out why any bid was rejected, and have access to a dispute settlement mechanism. In short, the entire procurement process must be made more open or transparent so that discrimination is made more difficult. The new government procurement code in the Tokyo Round attempts to do this. It contains detailed rules relating to such matters as describing the technical specifications for a product, publishing notices of bidding opportunities, qualifying as a possible supplier, determining the time allocated for submitting bids, awarding contracts, furnishing knowledge about bids, and reviewing complaints.

The code is clearly in the interests of the United States. The governments of most other industrial countries own or control a much larger part of secondary and tertiary economic activities than does the U.S. government. Moreover, the purchases of these industries often involve the type of high technology capital goods for which the United States has a competitive production advantage. While opportunities for trade worth as much as $20 billion a year could open up in foreign government purchasing markets now closed to U.S. exporters, there are still several important government agencies and classes of products excluded from the general provisions of the code. For example, most countries exclude telecommunications equipment, and the U.S. Defense Department omits such items as textiles, shoes, and specialty steel from its list of eligible products.

CUSTOMS VALUATION AND LICENSING

Two other areas where administrative practices sometimes restrict trade needlessly are valuing imports for the assessment of customs duties and issuing import licenses. The United States has nine different methods of determining customs value and has been severely criticized by foreign countries who charge that these methods are not applied in a uniform manner.

In addition, foreign governments argue that one of the nine methods, the so-called American selling price (ASP) is blatantly unfair. In the Tariff Act of 1922 some congressmen succeeded in raising the level of protection on a particular group of products of special interest to them not by raising the *rates* at which imports were taxed (since this would have made these rates embarrassingly high) but by raising the *base* on which the rates were levied.[7] Specifically, the duty was levied on the value of similar products produced in the United States rather than, as usual, on the export value of the items themselves. Suppose, for example, the selling price of a unit of some benzenoid chemical produced in the United States is $150, while the export value of the same commodity produced in Germany is $90. If a 40 percent tariff is levied on the American selling price, the duty is $60, whereas if levied on the export value, it is only $36. Under the ASP system the landed price of the foreign-produced chemical will, when transport costs are included, exceed the price of its American substitute. However, under the usual method of valuing imports, the foreign product will be cheaper if the various costs of shipping the product to the United States do not exceed $24, that is, $150 minus $90 minus $36. One of the few nontariff items negotiated in the Kennedy Round was the elimination of the ASP system, but Congress failed to accept this part of the package. If the new code on customs valuation is accepted by Congress, however, the ASP system will be abolished.

The new code sets out five methods of determining customs value. The first is the primary method, while the others are secondary methods to be followed in sequence if the primary method fails. The primary method values imports at their transaction value, that is "the price actually paid or payable for the goods when sold for export to the country of importation" plus certain costs and expenses incurred with respect to the imported goods that are not included in the price paid. Examples of these are selling commissions, brokerage fees, packing costs, royalties and license fees, and "assists," such as the plans or various tools that help the importer use or sell the product.

If the customs value cannot be ascertained under the primary method, the next method is to ascertain the transaction value of identical goods exported to the same country at or about the same time as the goods under consideration. The third method is to use the transaction value of similar (rather than identical) goods exported to the same country at the same time. Failing the existence of adequate information for this procedure, the importer can request that either the value be deduced from the unit price at which identical or similar goods imported at the same time are resold in the country of importation less appropriate transportation costs, profit margins, and the like, or be computed from material, manufacturing, and other costs and margins in the country of exportation. Both a committee on customs valuation consisting of the parties to the agreement and a technical committee on customs valuation under the auspices of the Customs Cooperation Council are established to facilitate dispute settlement. The customs valuation committee can request the technical committee to examine a disputed matter or create a panel for this purpose.

The transactions-value method is similar to the actual-value method that is cited in Article VII of the GATT as the preferred way of valuing imports for customs purposes. However, the growing practices of providing various services and assets free of charge or at reduced cost along with the product makes it necessary to elaborate how to calculate this value. Article VII merely states that, when the actual value cannot be determined, the value should be "based on the nearest ascertainable equivalent of such value." Spelling out in detail just what these other valuation methods are and the order in which they should be followed should go far in reducing the irritations of traders over customs valuation procedures.

Since U.S. exporters often complain that foreign customs officials arbitrarily increase the value of American products as well as that foreign customs procedures are uncertain, the new code deserves the support of Congress. Elimination of ASP is a concession in the technical sense of the word, but presumably this will be taken into account in determining the overall balance of concessions with other countries. As a customs valuation method, however, it deserves to be abolished, since it is deceitful in its purpose and grants a particular set of producers protective privilege that may no longer be warranted. Alternative, more transparent means for assistance exist, if these producers are being seriously injured or threatened with injury by imports.

Many countries, mainly developing nations, have import licensing systems for such purposes as facilitating the allocation of scarce foreign exchange. However, the red tape involved in obtaining these licenses sometimes makes them significant barriers to trade. An import licensing code, similar to those proposed for government procurement and customs valuation, tries to minimize any trade-distorting effects by specifying that the rules for submitting import-licensing applications be published, that the forms and procedures be as simple as possible, and that licenses not be refused for minor documentation errors or variations in value, quantity, or weight of the licensed product.

A section on automatic import licensing, that is, a system under which licenses are granted freely, states that import licensing should continue only "as long as the circumstances which gave rise to its introduction prevail" and that properly completed applications should be approved immediately on receipt or at least within a maximum of ten working days. In order to prevent discrimination among countries when licenses are not automatically issued, signatories agree to furnish information upon request concerning the past allocation by country and to publish the rules for applying for licenses as far in advance as possible of the opening date of submission. The period of license validity is not to be so short as to preclude imports, and governments are not to discourage the full utilization of quotas. In addition to dealing with other licensing technicalities that sometime distort trade, the code establishes a committee on import licensing to facilitate consultation and the settling of disputes.

Since 38 percent of U.S. industrial exports now go to developing countries, the reduction in delays and frustrations on the part of American exporters that this code promises should also be very much appreciated by the Congress.

The customs valuation and import licensing problems faced by exporters and importers are often child's play when compared with those arising from the many product standards with which these traders must contend. In customs valuation and import licensing, clearly identifiable governmental authorities issue regulations and make decisions. But product requirements relating to health, safety, environmental protection, national security, technology, packaging, marking and labeling, and the like are set out in many different places within the government and the private sector and are often difficult to discover by potential exporters or importers.

The standards code agreed upon by the negotiators states that technical regulations and certification procedures shall not be formulated or applied in a manner that creates obstacles to international trade or discriminates against the products of particular countries. To carry out these goals a series of procedures is agreed upon. When framing new standards and certification rules governments are to publish notices of this intent, provide copies of the proposed rules upon request, and allow enough time before their adoption for interested parties to comment upon them. Each adherent to the code shall ensure that "an enquiry point exists which is able to answer all reasonable enquiries from interested parties" regarding any technical regulation or certification system. Moreover, the signatories agree upon request to advise other members, especially the developing countries, on how best to meet their technical regulations.

There are two levels of obligations in carrying out these and other provisions in the code. For technical regulations and certification procedures set by central governments, the signatories "shall ensure that" these agencies comply with the code. For the various rules formulated by regional, state, local, and private organizations, the code requires its adherents to "take such reasonable means as may be available to them" to ensure compliance.

While encouraging the harmonization of standards among nations, the code is not intended to interfere with the right of countries to adopt rules that meet their particular goals in areas such as health, safety, and environmental protection. The dispute settlement mechanism is similar to that in the other codes. First, a member must enter into bilateral discussions if requested by another signatory. If the dispute is not resolved in these consultations, the matter can be referred to the committee on technical barriers to trade that is established under the code, which can then appoint technical expert groups or panels to consider the issues, consult with the disputants, and make recommendations or rulings on the matter. The committee reviews the finding of these groups and can authorize retaliatory actions.

Like the other technical codes, the one on standards represents a valuable attempt to reduce needless distortions of international trade. Furthermore, since the process of making rules and regulations is already more open in the United States than in many other countries, the efforts to publicize this process and to disseminate more widely knowledge about such rules is very much in U.S. interests.

With regard to trademarks and trade names U.S. negotiators have argued, not that rules and regulations are sometimes needlessly trade-distorting, but that more rules and regulations are needed to prevent "unfair" trade. Foreign producers sometimes affix the trademark or trade name of another firm on their products without permission. The United States has proposed discouraging this commercial counterfeiting by requiring that such merchandise be detained or seized at the time of importation, if the appropriate authorities are requested to do so by the person having the right to the protection of the trademark and trade name. Steps also would be taken to settle disputes and to prevent the misuse of this procedure to block imports. The reaction of other countries to the U.S. proposal has led to optimism that an agreement in this area can be reached within a few months.

SPECIAL AND DIFFERENTIAL TREATMENT FOR DEVELOPING COUNTRIES

Not only have the developing countries been accorded more favorable treatment in the tariff field by means of tariff preferences and exclusion from the full reciprocity requirement, but they have also been given special privileges in the various codes dealing with nontariff trade barriers. In the subsidies code, for example, developing countries are excluded from the ban on export subsidies, provided they agree "to reduce or eliminate export subsidies" when these are inconsistent with their "competitive needs." If they agree to this provision, other countries cannot take countervailing actions against their export subsidies in accordance with Article VI of GATT. However, developing country signatories also agree that their export subsidies shall not be used in a manner that causes adverse effects to the trade or production of another signatory, and action against these subsidies can be taken by resorting to the panel procedure under Articles XVI and XXIII. Similarly, the government procurement code permits developing countries to negotiate the exclusion of certain entities or products from the rules, while the safeguards code being considered contains a provision whereby the developed countries agree to make an effort to avoid safeguard actions on products of special interest to the developing nations. In addition to these special provisions, a general "enabling clause" has been agreed upon that provides a firmer legal basis for continuing tariff preferences and more favorable treatment with regard to nontariff trade barriers. Since this modifies the basic most-favored-nation principle set forth in Article I of the GATT, it was negotiated in the so-called Framework or GATT Reform Group. The clause merely states: "Notwithstanding the provisions of Article I in the General Agreement, contracting parties may accord differential and more favorable treatment to developing countries, without according such treatment to other contracting parties." This applies to tariffs, nontariff measures, regional or global arrangements among developing countries for reducing or eliminating tariffs, and special treatment for the least developed of the developing nations. The developed countries further agree not to expect reciprocal reductions in tariffs and nontariff barriers by the developing countries in trade negotiations if these are inconsistent with the developmental, financial, and trade needs of the latter countries. The text also contains the following clause dealing with the "graduation" of the developing countries to fuller GATT responsibilities:

> Less developed contracting parties expect that their capacity to make contributions or negotiated concessions or take mutually agreed upon action under the provisions and procedures of the General Agreement would improve with the progressive development of their economies and improvement in their trade situation and they would accordingly expect to participate more fully in the framework of rights and obligations under the General Agreement.

There is, however, no mechanism to determine when a developing country has reached the stage when it should assume these greater responsibilities. It has not been determined whether the text covering these points should appear as a new GATT article or be adopted by the members as a declaration or decision.

Safeguards for Balance of Payments and Development Purposes

Another issue considered by the Framework Group was measures taken for balance of payments and development purposes. The phrasing of Article XII dealing with restrictions to safeguard the balance of payments implies that, while quantitative controls over imports are permissible for this purpose, an import surcharge is not. However, countries have in fact quite often used this method, which most economists think is less distorting than quantitative restrictions. The declaration on the subject recognizes this fact and states that countries should use measures that are the least disruptive of trade. The signatories also declare their conviction that restrictive trade measures are in general an inefficient means of maintaining or restoring balance of payments equilibrium. The developing countries are also permitted in Article XVIII of the GATT to restrict imports for another purpose, namely, to implement their development programs. However, the provisions of the article are complex and quite stringent. The declaration broadens the reasons for taking such actions and makes them less difficult to meet.

Each of the major codes provides for a committee composed of the code's signatories to facilitate the settlement of disputes that have failed to be resolved through consultations between the disputants. Although the mechanisms differ somewhat from code to code, each committee elects its own chairman and can establish a panel of experts of from three to five members to review the facts of the case and make such findings as will assist the committee in making recommendations or giving rulings. The committee or a panel can also play a conciliating role in the dispute. Preference is given to government officials in selecting panel members from lists of qualified persons supplied by the signatories. After receiving the panel report the committee itself makes recommendations to the parties involved or rules on the matter. If the recommendations are not followed, the committee can take further appropriate action including, for example, the authorization of appropriate countermeasures. Some of the codes also specify that the committee keep under surveillance any matter on which it has made a recommendation or ruling.

In addition to the provisions in each code on dispute settlement, an Understanding Regarding Notification, Consultation, Dispute Settlement and Surveillance was agreed upon in the GATT Reform Group "with a view of improving and refining" the mechanism under Articles XXII (on consultation) and XXIII (on nullification or impairment). Under these articles the contracting parties (the entire GATT membership) rather than any committee appoint panels or working groups. receive the panel reports, make recommendations and rulings, and keep relevant matters under surveillance. The director-general proposes the composition of any panel to the contracting parties for approval. According to the understanding, members of a panel should "preferably be governmental." Moreover, while a panel "should make an objective assessment of the matter before it, including an objective assessment of the facts of the case and the applicability of and conformity with the General Agreement," it should make only such other findings as will assist the contracting parties in making recommendations or rulings "if so requested." Besides stating that the contracting parties shall keep under surveillance any matter on which they have made a recommendation or rule, the understanding includes a provision committing them "to conduct a regular and systematic review of developments in the trading system."

In evaluating the prospects for enforcing the various codes, it is necessary to consider why the panel procedure has not worked as well in recent years as in GATT's first decade.[8] Hudec points out that the fundamental reason is the breakdown in substantive consensus about GATT rules: some members feel that certain rules are no longer valid and that certain important trade problems are not covered in the document. The main purpose of negotiating new codes has been to amplify and modify the older GATT rules in order to meet these objections. Even if the new codes do handle these problems, however, it is still necessary to establish procedures that facilitate their enforcement. Although the basic intentions of the participants are good, they cannot be carried out unless the rules and procedures are framed so as to discourage partiality. In recent years governments have tended to regard complaints as hostile diplomatic acts and have exerted strong pressures on other governments not to activate the dispute settlement mechanism. Moreover, once panels have been established, pressures have been brought on their members—usually representatives of the different governments in GATT—for favorable findings or for settlement of the dispute prior to making such findings. In all of this the "big" trading powers have a considerable advantage over the developing nations and the smaller industrial countries. Consequently, as Hudec points out, "the pressures for compliance tend to vary according to the relative power of the governments involved, creating an inequitable situation in which the rules bind the weak but not the strong."[9]

Two steps to help prevent this outcome would be to enable the GATT secretariat itself to request the establishment of panels and to ensure that nongovernmental individuals are well represented on such panels. Unfortunately, the secretariat will not be allowed to activate the panel mechanism under the new codes or Article XXIII, and government officials will still be given preference as panel members. One cannot, therefore, help but wonder whether the same unsatisfactory procedures will continue by which many potential disputes never surface because of heavy-handed political and economic pressures or are smoothed over once they do surface rather than being settled on the basis of consistently applied rules. On the other hand, the creation of so many separate committees that can establish panels would seem to indicate that the GATT members at least expect many more disputes and panel decisions than in the recent past.

One part of the enforcement mechanism that is not likely to be very effective is that enabling the various committees to authorize retaliation or other appropriate action when their recommendations are not followed. Only once in its history has the GATT membership authorized retaliation.[10] Rather than trying to enforce panel decisions, the GATT membership has tended to accept a panel's decision and then to rely upon the resulting international pressures to secure compliance. Usually, the parties to the dispute have accepted the panel findings, although in a famous 1976 decision on tax practices relating to export subsidies neither the United States nor the other party to the dispute, the European Community, implemented the panel's decision. The fact of the matter is that governments are far from willing to yield the kind of authority that would make retaliation sanctioned by other GATT members an effective compliance measure. If retaliation is used too frequently, it is likely to push members into using pressures to block the formation of panels or into withdrawing from the various codes. Nonetheless, the dispute settlement procedure can be effective without this last step, provided the procedure is regularly utilized and the decisions are realistic yet impartial and well reasoned.

OECD STEEL COMMITTEE

An agreement reached outside the GATT framework but with important implications for the trade negotiations is the creation of a new International Steel Committee within the Organization of Economic Cooperation and Development (OECD). The committee's mandate states that governments need to work together not only to "ensure that trade in steel will remain as unrestricted and free of distortion as possible" and to "encourage reduction of barriers to trade" but "enable governments to act promptly to cope with crisis situations in close consultations with interested trading partners," to "facilitate needed structural adaptations . . . and promote rational allocation of productive resources," to "avoid encouraging economically unjustified investments," and to "facilitate multilateral cooperation consistent with the need to maintain competition, to anticipate and, to the extent possible, prevent problems." Among the committee's functions are following world supply and demand conditions in steel and developing "common perspectives" as well as establishing "where appropriate, multilateral objectives or guidelines for government policies."

The U.S. steel industry is reportedly pleased with the creation of this international committee. However, one must be somewhat concerned that the committee might turn into a cartel-like arrangement blocking needed adjustment in the industry and reducing its long-run efficiency.

AIRCRAFT AGREEMENT

Early in the Tokyo Round there was considerable hope for a series of sector negotiations in which the various tariffs and nontariff measures affecting a particular product line would be discussed within one group rather than among different groups organized on the basis of types of nontariff trade barriers. The only manufacturing area where such negotiations have been successful is the aircraft industry. Led by the United States, the participants have reached an agreement that frees trade on all civil aircraft and engines and on most parts and that commits the signatories to limit trade-restricting actions with regard to standards, government purchasing policies, quantitative restrictions, financing, and inducements. A committee on trade in civil aircraft is established for surveillance, consultation, and dispute settlement purposes. In view of the fact that U.S. dominance of the aircraft market is threatened by the announced intentions of the European Community, Canada, and Japan to build national aerospace industries of their own, this agreement should be widely appreciated in this country.

24

Agricultural trade barriers have long been among the most difficult to remove, for fairly obvious political reasons. The current negotiations have proved to be no exception to this general experience. Reportedly, tariff and nontariff concessions affecting almost $4 billion worth of U.S. agricultural exports (out of total agricultural exports of about $27 billion) were made by other countries. These cover meat, grain products, tobacco, fruit, vegetables, wine, nuts, and oilseed.

Agreements have also been reached on dairy products and bovine meat. These agreements establish councils for exchanging information about production and marketing conditions and for consultations among member representatives concerning world conditions and policies in these product areas. In addition, the dairy arrangement establishes minimum prices for milk powders, butter, milk fat, and cheese below which commercial trade is prohibited. An effort has also been made under the auspices of the United Nations Conference on Trade and Development (UNCTAD) to formulate a new wheat trade convention to replace the one expiring in June 1979. So far this has not succeeded. There are still disagreements over the size of the wheat reserves to be held as well as the prices at which to add and subtract from these reserves.

4

The Tariff-Cutting Formula

In the Kennedy Round negotiations the tariff-reducing rule finally agreed upon was a cut of 50 percent across the board, subject to a "bare minimum" of exceptions. (Of course, the fact that the average cut in manufactures came to 35 percent meant there was considerable slippage in the "bare minimum" notion.) The European Community (EC) pressed vigorously for a so-called harmonization formula whereby the higher the duty on an item, the greater the percentage cut in the duty. The United States opposed this approach for several reasons. The major one was the belief that, since all the harmonization formulas proposed by the EC resulted in a very modest average duty reduction, the EC was using this argument as a means of opposing a significant tariff reduction. Moreover, while there are good consumer-welfare reasons for reducing high duties a greater percentage, it seemed unfair to subject producers in high-duty industries to considerably greater pressures from import competition than producers in low-duty industries. The high-duty industries are often precisely the ones where the difficulties of adjustment for labor and capital are the greatest. Congress recognized this fact by allowing cuts of up to 100 percent for tariffs of 5 percent or below but of only 50 percent for duty rates above 5 percent. Furthermore, a constant percentage cut already puts high-duty industries under somewhat greater import pressure than low-duty industries. Suppose, for example, that the international prices of two products are fixed at $100 each, and the import duty on one is 50 percent while on the other 10 percent. When the first good is imported, it will sell for $150 in the domestic market (ignoring transport and other costs), whereas the other good will sell domestically for $110 when imported. Cutting the duty 50 percent on each will reduce the selling price on the first product to $125, or by 16.7 percent, and on the second to $105, or by only 4.5 percent.

In the Tokyo Round negotiations the United States proposed a tariff-cutting formula of 60 percent across the board. (This was the maximum cutting authority permitted under the 1974 Trade Act, although again duties of 5 percent or less could be completely eliminated.) The European Community countered with a harmonization formula. Specifically, the percentage cut in each duty would be the level of the duty itself. Moreover, the process would be repeated four successive times to reach the final rate. For example, a 40 percent duty would be cut by 40 percent to 24 percent. This would then be cut 24 percent to 18.2 percent; the 18.2 percent figure would be reduced by 18.2 percent to 14.9 percent. This would finally be cut by 14.9 percent to 12.7 percent. While for high duties the cut under this formula would be greater than the 60 percent proposal of the United States, the average cut on all dutiable items would amount to only about 30 percent.

In various simulations the United States discovered that with likely exceptions the employment and trade effects from a given average percentage cut achieved through harmonization formulas were actually somewhat more favorable for this country than those resulting from a uniform cut. In view of the strong position taken by the EC on the issue and the absence of real enthusiasm in this country for a significant cut such as 60 percent, the United States tentatively agreed to the harmonization approach provided the average cut was considerably greater than the EC's formula yielded. The final formula agreed upon was proposed by the Swiss. The rate at which a duty is cut is the rate of duty itself divided by the duty rate plus 0.14. Thus, the rate at which a 30 percent duty would be cut is $0.30/(0.30 + 0.14) = 0.68$ or 68 percent. There is no economic rationale for the particular formula. It was selected from among others because it gave an average cut of about 40 percent (before exceptions) and most governments found the degree of harmonization acceptable. The United States is constrained somewhat in following the formula in that it cannot reduce any tariff above 5 percent by more than 60 percent. However, it can—and did—reduce duties 5 percent or below by more than this percentage in order to raise its average cut after exceptions to a level comparable to that of the other major participants. The average percentage cut on dutiable manufactures that will be made by the United States is 31 percent.

As one who was involved in the harmonization hassle in the Kennedy Round, I can only express admiration at the ability of the Tokyo Round technicians to sell to their more practical-minded superiors and to private business and labor groups an esoteric formula like $t/(t + 0.14)$ (where t is the tariff rate) as the tariff-reducing rule for the Multilateral Trade Negotiations. Moreover, one wonders why industries that must, for example, accept a 59 percent cut in their protective tariff because the level of this duty is 20 percent do not object to the undue burden when they observe a duty cut of only 42 percent in industries protected by a 10 percent tariff. Perhaps such factors as the fairly low levels of most duties, the eight-to-ten-year stretchout period for the duty reductions, and recent fluctuations in exchange rates that dwarf these tariff cuts have greatly diminished the concerns of various economic groups over the exact nature of the tariff reductions affecting them.

There is understandable concern by legislators over the possible adverse employment effects of the tariff reductions. However, detailed studies of these effects indicate not only that the overall employment impact is likely to be extremely small but that instances of adverse regional or industry effects can generally be easily absorbed through normal labor turnover and market growth in the region or industry as well as by staging the cuts over eight to ten years. My own simulation of a 50 percent reduction (with certain product exceptions) yields a net impact on total employment of only —15,000 jobs or about 2/100 of 1 percent of the labor force.[11] Studies by Deardorff and Stern and by Cline and others estimate the aggregate employment impact of a 50 percent cut at —24,000 and +24,000 jobs, respectively.[12]

Regional and occupational effects are also quite small. For example, the labor impact in New England—the region which incurs the largest net loss, according to my calculations—is only —3,000 jobs. When one considers that this number is based on a 50 percent rather than a 30 percent reduction, that a major import-sensitive New England industry (footwear) included in the 50 percent calculations is in fact being excluded from any duty reductions, and finally that the cuts will be staged over at least eight years, the conclusion can only be that this (or any other) region should not be concerned about adverse employment effects from the Tokyo Round tariff reductions.

Since there is much evidence that the U.S. comparative advantage position in international trade is based on a relatively abundant supply of human capital and an ability to create new technology, it is not surprising that the demand for highly skilled workers tends to increase whereas that for comparatively unskilled workers tends to decline as a result of a multilateral tariff reduction. These effects are, however, again very small. My estimates are that a 50 percent cut would tend to increase employment of those involved in research and development by 14/100 of 1 percent and of other professional and technical workers by 8/100 of 1 percent. On the other hand, the initial impact on semiskilled and unskilled production workers is an employment decline of 14/100 of 1 percent and 8/100 of 1 percent, respectively, in the number employed in these skill groups. However, the estimates do show that certain industries in which recent market growth has been low or negative could be faced with a considerable adjustment problem when faced with a 50 percent duty reduction. These include certain textile products not subject to quotas, nonrubber footwear, electronic tubes, glass products, ceramic tiles, pottery products, and primary lead and zinc.

The response to these occupation and industry figures should not be to demand that no duty cuts producing these results be made but rather to try to ensure that adjustment takes place in a noninjurious manner. Reciprocal duty reductions afford the country one of its few opportunities of moving to a higher living standard in a predictable and controllable manner. (Just the static net welfare gain to the nation of a 50 percent reciprocal cut is estimated at over $1 billion.)[13] By combining active adjustment assistance policies with less-than-formula cuts and longer staging periods, affected workers can be shifted either to higher earning positions or, if necessary, be protected until they voluntarily leave or retire. The preferred approach is to use adjustment assistance policies, but unfortunately our programs in this field are still quite primitive and lack political support from labor. Consequently, the administration has used the technique of either excluding from duty cuts most of the above industries or reducing tariffs in these sectors only modestly. While this is a second-best approach, it should at least eliminate any credible charges that the actual duty reductions will cause appreciable injury to any industry or occupational group.

Notes to Text

[1] See section 151 of Public Law 93-618. The President's notice to Congress of his intention to enter into trade agreements and a summary of various provisions may be found in the *Federal Register*, vol. 44 (January 8, 1979), p. 1933.

[2] See Richard Blackhurst, Nicolas Marian, and Jan Tumlir, *Trade Liberalization, Protectionism, and Interdependence*, GATT Studies in International Trade, no. 5 (Geneva: General Agreement on Tariffs and Trade, November 1977).

[3] The contracting parties are the members of the GATT acting in a collective manner.

[4] Robert E. Hudec, *The GATT Legal System and World Trade Diplomacy* (New York: Praeger Publishers, 1975), appendix A; and Robert E. Hudec, *Adjudication of International Trade Disputes*, Thames Essay no. 16 (London: Trade Policy Research Centre, 1978), pp. 5-6, n. 2.

[5] 41 U.S.C. 10a–10d.

[6] Robert E. Baldwin, *Nontariff Distortions of International Trade* (Washington, D.C.: Brookings Institution, 1970), pp. 70-78.

[7] The products now covered are benzenoid chemicals, rubber-soled footwear, canned clams, and certain knit gloves.

[8] Hudec, *Adjudication of International Trade Disputes*, p. 11.

[9] Ibid., p. 3.

[10] Ibid., p. 82.

[11] Robert E. Baldwin and Wayne E. Lewis, "U.S. Tariff Effects on Trade and Employment in Detailed SIC Industries" in William G. Dewald, ed., *The Impact of International Trade and Investment on Employment* (Washington, D.C.: U.S. Department of Labor, 1978).

[12] Alan V. Deardorff and Robert M. Stern, "A Disaggregated Model of World Production and Trade," presented to a conference on Micro Modeling for International Trade Policy, University of Western Ontario, London, Ontario, February 23-24, 1979, processed; and W. Cline, N. Kawanabe, T. Kronsjo, and T. Williams, *Trade Negotiations in the Tokyo Round* (Washington, D.C.: Brookings Institution, 1978).

[13] Robert E. Baldwin, John H. Mutti, and J. David Richardson, "Welfare Effects in the United States of a Significant Multilateral Tariff Reduction," Department of Economics, University of Wisconsin-Madison, April 1978, processed.